Iwokrama Mission Statement

The aim of Iwokrama is to promote the conservation and sustainable and equitable use of tropical rain forests in a manner that will lead to lasting ecological, economic and social benefit to the people of Guyana and to the world in general.

'One day when there are no trees left, the heavens will fall and all men will be destroyed.'

An Amerindian saying

Foreword by His Royal Highness, The Prince of Wales

As Patron of the Iwokrama International Centre of Rain Forest Conservation and Development in Guyana, I have been one of the lucky ones to visit the Iwokrama Forest and experience for myself the astonishing variety and exuberance of the rain forest and the friendly welcome of the people who depend upon it for their livelihoods.

Tropical rain forests, home to over half of the world's plants and animals, cover a mere six percent of the planet, and yet their value in terms of global goods and services is only now beginning to be understood fully. With more than half of the world's tropical forests already converted to non-forest uses, a more equitable, sustainable approach to rain forest management is urgently required.

Within this context, Iwokrama stands for an international ideal. Few projects capture the imagination as Iwokrama does with its holistic and innovative approaches to this global problem. Over the past four years, it has emerged as a centre for excellence in sustainable development practice. It has taken up, with courage and energy, the challenge of demonstrating that rain forest daily use and long-term conservation can go hand in hand. This achievement would not have been possible without the help and support of a diverse range of supporters, from the international, national, and local communities, from scientists and businessmen to schoolchildren and film-makers.

The American-born, British-based artist, Shirley Felts, reflects that strength of support from so many people. She first came to Guyana in 1999 as a tourist. Her brief stay in the Iwokrama Forest extended for several weeks and became an annual visit. Many Iwokrama supporters know her paintings as they have been used as illustrations in Iwokrama publications and on cards. Now this book provides a delightful perspective on Iwokrama that enriches our perceptions of the rain forest and excites our imagination. Her rich palette of artistic skills lends itself to the spectacular array of colours, shapes and sights seen within the world of the tropical rain forest. I hope that this book inspires you with its beauty and its message of fragility....

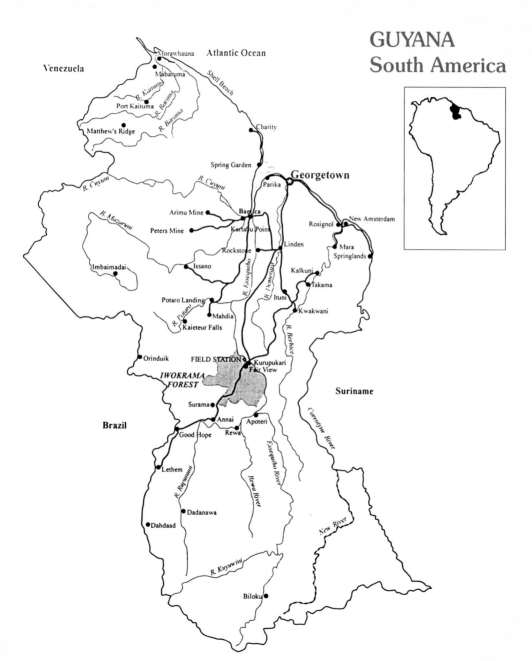

GUYANA
South America

Atlantic Ocean

Venezuela

Morawhauna
Mabaruma
R. Kaituma
Port Kaituma
R. Barima
R. Barima
Matthew's Ridge

Shell Beach

Charity

Spring Garden

Georgetown

Parika

R. Cuyuni
R. Cuyuni

Arimu Mine
Bartica
Kartabu Point

Rosignol

New Amsterdam

Peters Mine
R. Mazaruni

Rockstone

Linden

Mara
Springlands

Imbaimadai

Issano

Kalkuni

Takama

Potaro Landing
R. Essequibo
R. Demerara

Ituni

Kwakwani

R. Potaro

Mahdia
Kaieteur Falls

Orinduik
FIELD STATION
Kurupukari
Fair View

IWOKRAMA
FOREST

R. Berbice

Suriname

Surama
Annai
Apoteri

Brazil

Good Hope
Rewa

Corentyne River

Lethem

R. Rupununi

Essequibo River

Rewa River

New River

Dadanawa

Dahdaad

R. Kuyuwini

Biloku

Preface by His Excellency Bharrat Jagdeo
President of the Republic of Guyana

In 1989, Guyana made one of the most tangible contributions yet towards the global effort to demonstrate how tropical rain forest can be sustainably and equitably used without depriving the people who depend on these forests of its ecological, social and economical benefits. In the heart of Guyana, nearly one million acres or 370,000 ha of pristine tropical rain forest was made available to the international community to be used as an experimental centre to develop sustainable forest management models for application elsewhere.

After a long gestation, the Iwokrama International Centre for Rain Forest Conservation and Development was established in 1996 and a programme started that focuses on meaningful pluralistic partnerships at the local, national, regional and international levels. Over the past few years, it has become a bridge between many approaches and ideas, just as Guyana is the bridge between the Caribbean and the Latin American countries of South America. As a culture founded firmly in diversity, Guyana's strength lies in being able to bridge these contrasts. Hence it gives me great pleasure to see this publication on Iwokrama as another bridge, as a work that links science and art. This book enables us to consider not only the scientific discoveries and social development that has emerged from the Iwokrama Forest Programme but also the aesthetic beauty of the forest and the inspiration for the artist, Shirley Felts.

Shirley Felts has captured the regal majesty of several endangered species that can be found in Iwokrama in relative abundance, including black caiman, harpy eagle, jaguar, and giant otter. Their diverse habitats are captured in vignettes of the shadowy forest and the serenity of the riversides. These illustrations will be the source of joy for many who will never have the opportunity to visit a tropical rain forest to experience the real glory and biodiversity richness such forests possess and will be a tangible memory over the years for those who do visit. It is my hope also that this book would be source of inspiration to many, particularly Guyanese artists, to emulate her effort, not only in capturing the richness of nature that lies around them, but also to develop the discipline and strength of character that are so evident in her work. Welcome to Iwokrama, the heart of Guyana as seen through the eyes of an artist.

Bharrat Jagdeo
President of the Republic of Guyana

For Vanda, Colin and Gertrude

I wish to express my gratitude to Iwokrama's Director Generals – Kathryn Monk, David Cassells and Henry Tschinkel. Sincere thanks to Vanda Radzik and to the many people in the Iwokrama Centre in Georgetown who made possible, over the years, my visits to the rain forest. I could not have put this book together without the financial support of the Canadian International Development Agency (CIDA) for which I am deeply grateful.

Thanks to Fred Alicock and the staff at Kurupukari Field Station who guided and assisted me in every way and who provided good meals. Thanks to the people of Fair View Village who welcomed me and tolerated my whole days of painting there. Thanks to my friends, Gertrude Fredericks of Aranaputa Valley and Valerie Cox from South Rupununi who, with the Embroidery Group, introduced me to Makushi Indian folklore and myths through their sensitive work. Colin and Velda Edwards of Rock View Lodge at Annai gave comfort and hospitality when passing to and from the Field Station.

Special thanks to my husband, Derek, and my children, Nicholas, Martin and Katy, for their patience and encouragement and to Wayne Price for her great interest in Iwokrama's mission and her supporting gift. Thanks to James Butler, Nick Mulhern, Chris Mulhern and Gordon Duncan who helped in different ways.

THE IWOKRAMA RAIN FOREST

Illustrations and words by Shirley Felts

Iwokrama International Centre for Rain Forest Conservation and Development
Guyana, South America

Published in 2003 by
Iwokrama International Centre
for Rain Forest Conservation
and Development
67 Bel Air
Georgetown, Guyana,
South America
tel: (592) 225-1504 Fax (592) 225-59199
Email: iwokrama@iwokrama.org

Printed by BAS Printers
in Great Britain

I.S.B.N. 976 8120 03 7

The Iwokrama International Rain Forest Programme, inaugurated by the Government and People of Guyana through the initiative of former President – the late Mr. Hugh Desmond Hoyte, was launched under Commonwealth auspices in 1989, using nearly a million acres of pristine tropical rain forest for research, training and environmental purposes, to demonstrate how the world's forests can be conserved and utilised in a sustainable way.

A field station has been established on the west bank of the Essequibo river and is managed by Amerindian staff, whose traditional knowledge of the forest is essential for research and our own survival.

The Iwokrama field station at Kurupukari.

The Hoatzin is Guyana's national bird.

Making our way down river to the field station.

About a mile up river from the field station is the attractive village of Fair View. In addition to their staple food, cassava, the people here grow fruit such as coconuts, limes, oranges, mangoes, bananas and the fruit of the manicole palm, their seeds being dispersed by wild birds and mammals.

Errol McBirney's pet macaw.

Sarah George's house in a clearing with her chickens and lazy dog.

The Essequibo River and Peter's Island at Fair View, the waterfall, cat fish, arapaima, caiman, piranha, anaconda, electric eel, sawfish, rays, needle fish . . .

Flowering heliconias,
dense vegetation and – high
in the canopy – glimpses
of red flowering vines,
brightly coloured birds,
monkeys . . .
Great palms and rubber trees,
moras, huge domed ceibas.
Everything is alive.

Echoing song of quadrilles,
screaming pihas.
Heavy vines, slender vines,
delicate fronds.

Brilliant green vegetation. Huge trees, huge leaves – the hum of the forest and occasional screams and clattering. The haunting sound of howler monkeys, flittings of colourful butterflies and humming birds.

Up river, a giant turtle laying her eggs in the red sand.

Following the Field Station's "Screaming Piha" trail, echoing sounds swell out from the forest; tree frogs, cries of parrots, eerie flutterings and the steady chittering of cicadas. Kingfishers, orioles, macaws, trogons, toucans, Cock of the Rock – birds flash across and above.

*So much heard
but not seen.*

Wild fig, philodendron,
coatis running in pairs,
parrots hurrying down the sky.

*The canoe enters a side channel
under lianas and flowering vines, backed by
brilliant vegetation. A shelter near the bank.*

Heliconias, epiphytes –
humming birds hovering over
the flowering lianas.
Armadillos and occasional
sightings of monkeys.
A jaguar lurks nearby.

A profusion of flowering vines, leaves, everything twisting, turning and climbing.

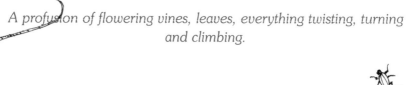

In the Rupununi Savannah: creeks fingering out from rivers; giant water lilies, giant otters, caiman, kaboura flies, shocking, primeval green iguanas

and curious tapirs.

33

Massive trees with great
buttress roots, ages old,
wrapped with vines and thorn
trees and guarded
by armies of ants, beetles,
hornets . . .

Mist rising from the river, still night, we hear crickets, then chirping tree frogs and bats whizzing overhead. Birds break through with their own dawn chorus.

Stars sprinkle down on all sides

List of animals illustrated

Heron (*Ardea sp.*) pg 25
Nine Banded Armadillo (*Dasypusa novemcintus*) pg 28
Jaguar (*Panthera onca*) pg 28, 29
Black Spider Monkey (*Ateles paniscus*) pg 29
Ameiva ameiva pg 30
Insects (butterflies, fruit bugs, beetles, stick insects) pg 31
Giant otter (*Pteronura brasiliensis*) pg 32
Salipenter pg 30
Tapir (*Tapisur terrestris*) pg 33
Fart frog (*Phyllomedusa bicolor*) pg 39

compiled by: Hemcranauth Sambhu, Christopher Chin, Deirdre Jaferally
Iwokrama Research Assistants, Wildlife unit

Rain Forest flora

Orchids 193 known species
Plants   6101 known species
Trees   1000 species

List of endangered species in the Iwokrama Forest, Cites 1

Family	Species	Common
Dasypodidae	*Priodontes maximus*	Giant Armadillo
Myrmecophagidae	*Myrmecophaga tridactyla*	Giant Anteater
Canidae	*Speothos venaticus*	Bush Dog
Felidae	*Leopardus pardalis*	Ocelot
Felidae	*Leopardus tigerinus*	Oncilla
Felidae	*Leopardus wiedii*	Margay
Felidae	*Panthera onca*	Jaguar
Mustelidae	*Lontra longicaudis*	South American River Otter
Mustelidae	*Pteronura brasiliensis*	Giant River Otter
Ciconiidae	*Jabiru mycteria*	Jabiru Stork
Accipitridae	*Harpia harpyja*	Harpy Eagle
Psittacidae	*Ara macao*	Scarlet Macaw
Alligatoridae	*Melanosuchus niger*	Black Caiman
Pelomedusidae	*Podocnemis unifilis*	Yellow-spotted River Turtle
Pelomedusidae	*Podocnemis expansa*	South American River Turtle
Testudinidae	*Geochelone denticulata*	Yellow-footed Tortoise

All the paintings have been done in situ – in the forest and along the river and savannah, with the exception of those painted back in the studio – elements of the Guyana rain forest experience; pages 5, 24, 29, 38 and the jacket illustration.